A Newbies Guide to FileMaker 11 Pro

A Beginners Guide to Database Management

Minute Help Guides

www.minutehelp.com

Table of Contents

Chapter 1: Introduction

FileMaker Pro is an easy-to-use database management tool with powerful applications for both professional and personal tasks. From contacts and documents to inventory management and invoicing, FileMaker Pro makes it easy to share and manage data with an entire team. In addition to business project and file management, FileMaker Pro can also help manage personal assets, photography, and other creative files.

FileMaker Pro comes with a PDF manual and an impressive collection of online help documents. These resources are extremely helpful – if you're an advanced user. If you're a new user, this guide will walk you through the first steps for getting started and familiarizing yourself with the program.

This guide will explain the basic principles behind FileMaker, including the fundamental differences between a spreadsheet and database. We'll provide step-by-step instructions for how users can ask and solve problems, view the same data in several different ways, link related data (via a relational table or database) and share data over the Internet (via a web database). Most importantly, we'll let you know which features are important – and which you can worry about at a later date.

Chapter 2: Overview of FileMaker

2.1 FileMaker Basics

What is a database?

A database is a collection of information that solves a problem. It can be as simple as a phone book, or as complex as companywide procurement system. The basic building blocks of a database are fields, records and files. Using the phone book example, a *field* is a single piece of information, such as a name or number. A record can contain multiple fields. For example, your *record* in the phonebook will contain your name, number and address. The phone book itself is a *file*, containing all the records for a specific region.

A spreadsheet, in contrast, is a flat storage system for information. Think of it as a little calculator. You can enter numbers and perform functions to calculate the relationships between these numbers. That's all well and good, but in order to find any information contained in your spreadsheet, you'll have to do so yourself. A database, on the other hand, will find it for you.

FileMaker is a computer program that helps you build a database to organize and access the information you need exactly when you need it. It can handle large amounts of data, let people share this data across multiple computers and provides an interface for accessing, organizing and searching the data.

What's the difference between FileMaker and MySQL?

MySQL is an open-source database program that simply holds data. It's extremely powerful and used by computer programmers who build sophisticated structures to interface with this data. FileMaker Pro, however, is a desktop database. It's a single piece of software that works for both users and developers. FileMaker uses simple concepts, like "find", "sort" and "connect". There's no confusing "query" or "alias" jargon to learn, and you don't need a computer science degree to understand FileMaker. In fact, with this guide, we'll help you hit the ground running – no experience required!

Can FileMaker interface with MySQL?

Absolutely. FileMaker Pro can also be used as a "front end" program for MySQL, creating a streamlined interface for interacting with complex data.

2.2 Getting Started

When you first launch FileMaker, you'll see a screen that looks like this:

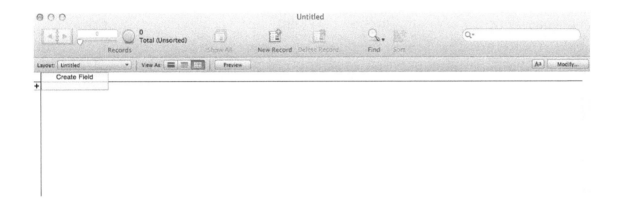

- **Content Area** – Your data goes here.
- **Scroll bars** – Use these to resize the viewing window
- **Zoom controls** – Zoom in for a closer look, zoom out for the bigger picture
- **Mode pop-up menu** – Switch between different viewing modes
- **Status tool bar** – These tools set changes based on your current mode; for example, in Browser mode you can use the 'New Record' button to input data, while in Find mode you can create 'Find Requests' to locate data.

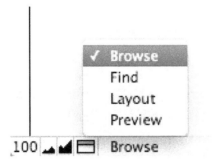

Using the mode pop-up menu to switch between the different viewing modes

Every FileMaker database comes with two main features: the data itself, and the tools you use to interact with this data. There are also four viewing modes for helping you view, edit and manage your data:

Browse: Add, change and view data; it's the mode where you'll spend most of your time, and also the default mode whenever you launch FileMaker

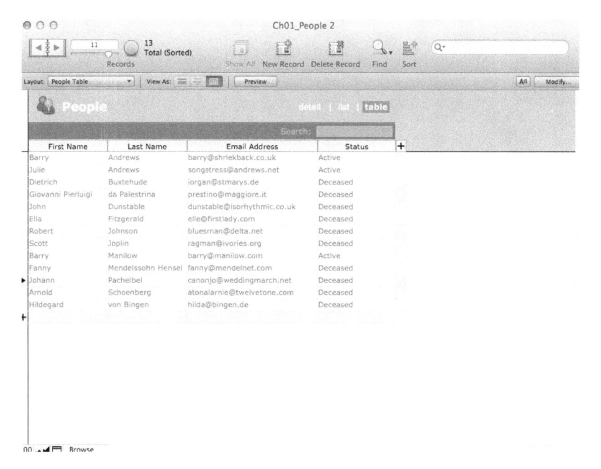

Browse mode in table view; select detail or list at the top to switch views

Find: Tell FileMaker what you need to locate and Find mode will do the dirty work

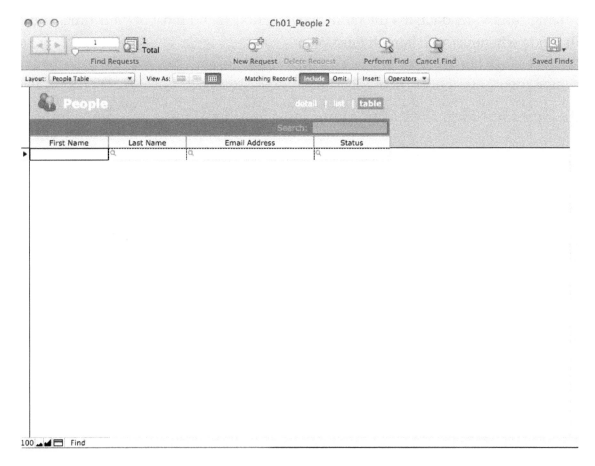

Find mode

Layout: Build the elements of your database, including designing difference layouts for interfacing with your data

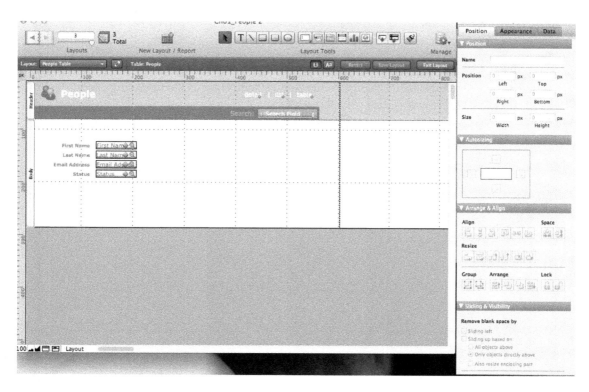

Layout mode with the Inspector open

Preview: Need to print something? Click this for a one-page-at-a-time view of your data, exactly as it will look when printed

Preview mode; switch between detail, list and table at the top to see how each view will look when printed

2.3 New Features for FileMaker 11:

If you've used FileMaker before, you'll notice there are several key additions to FileMaker 11:

- **FileMaker Charts** – Take your data to a whole new level with three-dimensional charts; another reason to say goodbye to Excel – bar charts, pie charts, line charts (virtually EVERY chart) is built right into FileMaker.

- **Quick Reports in a Spreadsheet** – Create quick reports in a spreadsheet to get even more out of your data

- **QuickFind** – With no programming necessary, users can easily add a "QuickFind" box to their toolbar, using it to search every field in the current layout instantaneously (yes, it's that easy: see 3.4)

- **Instant web publishing** – Your online databases will work and look just like FileMaker Pro on your desktop

- **Recurring import** – Regularly import files? Recurring import makes this easy. (4.2)

2.4 Bento v. FileMaker

If you use FileMaker or are just getting started, you may also have heard of Bento. Think of Bento as FileMaker's MUCH younger sister. When FileMaker was first created in 1985, Bento was not even a figment of a developer's imagination. Bento, a Mac-only program that was first introduced in 2008, is designed to take data from iCal, Address Book and Mail and create a database. Like the tidy Japanese lunchbox that the program takes it name from, Bento creates a basic database for organizing your data. It's just for the single user, however, and does not allow database sharing.

Should I use Bento or FileMaker?

If you have a Mac and only need to manage personal contacts, then Bento may be all you ever need. If you have more complex needs – like tracking inventory, managing financial records and billing, AND managing contacts, you'll want to use FileMaker. Additionally, if you want to share your database with other uses, you'll need to use FileMaker as well. Finally, if you have a PC, you don't have much of a choice – your only option is FileMaker. (That's not a bad thing!)

Chapter 3: Working with a Database

Ready to build your first database? We'll help you put theory to practice, build some calculations to think for you, scripts to do your grunt work, and show you how to transform a flat database into a powerful relational one.

3.1 Adding data

Whether you're adding addresses or test grades, FileMaker thinks of each piece of information as a field. Related fields are then grouped into records. For example, a student at a school would be a record, and each of her test scores would be a field in that record. The entire student body would be the database. FileMaker allows you to create an infinite number of fields for each record. Every record in the database will have the same fields, although you don't have to add information to every field.

When you first get started with an empty database, you'll add a record. First, be sure you are in Browse Mode. Next, select Choose Records -> New Record or Ctrl (⌘) + N. Using our school example, you'll enter the name of a student. Next, you'll create fields to hold information that's relevant. To save a record, you'll need to commit it. Simply click outside the record box or hit Enter/Return on your keypad, and the record will be committed to your database.

TIP: Add data efficiently. The last thing you want to do is waste precious time clicking from field to field. Use these shortcuts to streamline the process:

- Tab: Move to the next field
- Shift+Tab: Move to the previous field

TIP: Use conditional formatting to track data as you enter it into the database. For example, you can choose to have fields in your database shaded yellow as you enter information so you stay oriented to where you're typing. See 4.4 for managing conditional formatting.

3.2 Editing data

It's just as easy to edit your data as it is to enter it. Simply select a record, click the field that needs to be updated and enter the new information. You can only be in one record at any given moment; the record you are using is appropriately called the "Active" record. When you edit a record, the fields will appear with a dotted line around them. When you make edits to a record, you'll also see a field called "Modified Changes".

What if I make a mistake when editing?

If you still have the record open, select Records -> Revert Record. You can only use the revert command when you've got the record open and are actively editing it. If you've already committed the changes, you won't be able to revert. The same goes if someone else made the edit; you can't use revert to change it back.

How can I duplicate a record?

Do you have multiple records to enter that share virtually all the same information? One of the fastest ways to add this data is by duplicating one record and then tweaking the fields. To do this, select Records -> Duplicate and FileMaker will copy everything over in the duplicate. If your database is unsorted, you'll find your new duplicated record at the end of the database, not next to the original.

How do I delete a record?

To delete a record, choose Records -> Delete Record. You'll need to confirm your intention to delete the record, and then FileMaker will remove the record you are currently on. You can also use the Find command to select multiple records. Once these are all selected, choose Records -> Delete Found Records. To remove every record in your database, select Records -> Show All Records, and then choose Records -> Delete All Records. Ciao!

3.3 Navigating your records

From the Browse mode, click on the book icon to flip through each record as though it were a page in a book. The status bar at the bottom will tell you which record you are currently viewing and how many more records there are in your file. Use the slider to speed read your book, sliding quickly to the middle, end or back to the beginning.

Know which record you need to be on? Simply type in the record number to quickly jump to it. As a word of caution, record numbers are ephemeral creatures. They change as you add, delete or sort records. So don't bother memorizing them. If you want to remember records based on a number, you can assign a serial number. We'll discuss that in 3.7.

TIP: Use keyboard shortcuts to make record navigation painless.

- Next Record: Ctrl + Down Arrow
- Pervious Record: Ctrl + Up Arrow
- Activate current record indicator: ESC, then record number and Enter/Return
- Move from one field to the next: Tab (NOTE: To indent a line, type CTRL + Tab)

3.4 Finding your records

Use Find mode to quickly locate any record or a group of records. There are four ways to access Find mode:

- Mode pop-up menu: Find
- View -> Find mode
- Status toolbar -> Find tool
- Ctrl + F

In Find mode, each field displays a magnifying glass as a friendly reminder that you're entering in search criteria, not new information. The status toolbar has also changed; you'll notice the "Perform Find" and "Saved Find" options are now available. When you enter search criteria, you are making what FileMaker calls a "request". FileMaker can save these request descriptions under "Saved Find" to make it easier to locate needed records in the future.

You'll make a request the same way that you enter information in Browse mode. Simply select the correct field and enter your requested data (e.g., last name, telephone number, zip code) and all corresponding records will appear. Once you conduct a search, FileMaker switches back to browse mode so you can view and edit your records. You'll only be able to view the records that FileMaker found. To see omitted records, select the Records -> Show Omitted Only or click the pie chart.

What if Find doesn't show what I need?

You'll need to modify your search. Do so by choosing Records -> Modify Find. This will take you back to Find mode and display your last request. Do NOT simply click Find mode. This will clear your previous search, so you'll have to start all over again.

What is FastMatch?

FastMatch lets your find records with matching data instantly. Let's say you need every record with an address based in California. The record that you're currently viewing is from California. Drag to select "California" from your current record and then right click on your selected text. Select Find matching records from the pop-up menu, and you'll see every contact in your address book that has a California address.

What is QuickFind?

Like FastMatch, QuickFind instantly shows every record that matches your search criteria. Even better, you don't need to be in a specific record to make QuickFind work. From the right side of the toolbar, simply type your word or phrase, hit Enter, and you'll see every matching record.

Why am I seeing a 'No Records Match' error message?

FileMaker displays this when nothing matches your search. Chances are, you've misspelled your search criteria, or you've misspelled your term in the actual record. Try typing part of the word to see if you can turn up the record in question.

3.5 Using View mode

View mode allows you to organize and edit records, allowing you to sort, move and shape your information in sophisticated ways. There are three main ways to view your data:

Form view – One record at a time

List view – All your records; use the scroll bar to swipe through them

Table view – View your records as a spreadsheet with one row for each record and one column for each field

How do I customize Table view?

To switch between views, use the View menu. Table view is most convenient for viewing large amounts of data at once. You can also modify which data you see while in this view. To do so, from the Status toolbar select the Modify button. Check/uncheck boxes to change which fields are visible. You can also drag field names to rearrange the order. To further customize Table view, select View -> Layout Mode and select the Layout Setup dialog. This gives you full control over everything from critical details to aesthetic design preferences. We'll discuss more Layout editing options in 4.3.

To manage options like resizing columns or clickable sorting of column headers, select the Table View Properties. Making changes to table view properties will also affect how your table prints. Controlling how you view your data is just one of the many customization options available to you in FileMaker.

3.6 Calculations that think for you

FileMaker is designed to make your life easier, and calculation fields can help. Let's say your database stores information about your clients, including how much your clients spend each month. What if you want to figure out the total amount of money your client has spent with your business? You could add up every month's expenditures, but that would be a tedious process, and you'd need to repeat the process for every client every month. With a calculation field, FileMaker will do this for you.

1. Select File -> Manage -> Database and click the "Fields" tab.
2. In the field name, type "Total Spend"
3. From the Type pop-up menu, select "Calculation"
4. Choose Create
5. For this specific calculation, it's based on the monthly spend.
6. Select the first month, type the "+" sign, select the next month, and so on.
7. From the calculation result pop-up menu select 'Number'
8. Click ok to save.

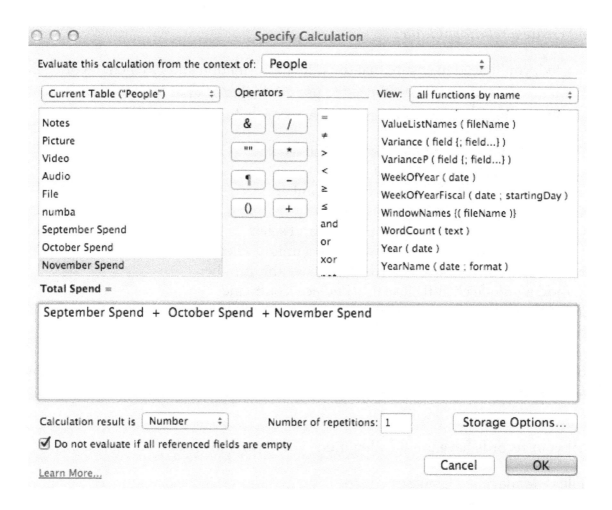

NOTE: If you don't see your new calculation field immediately appear, don't panic. Depending on your viewing preferences, you may be unable to see new fields. Simply switch to Layout mode and be sure the field can be viewed. Switch back to Browse mode and you'll see your calculation.

3.7 Working with relational data

What is relational data?

A table holds information about one type of thing, such as your Client Information table or Monthly Payment table. Within one database, it's possible to have multiple tables. A relationship describes how the records in two different tables relate to each other. Most relationships are parent-child; a parent record can have multiple children, but a child record can have only one parent. In this example, the parent is the Client Information table, while each payment that your client makes is a child.

How do I create a relational table?

To get started, you'll need to ensure that the Client Information and Payment records are properly matched. To do so, you will need to use FileMaker's Serial Number option. This automatically assigns a unique number to every record when it's created.

1. File -> Manage -> Database, click the 'Fields' tab
2. In the field name, type clientID
3. From the Type pop-up menu, choose number
4. Click Create
5. Click the Options button for "clientID" and select "Serial number"; now every record you create in your client table will have a unique clientID number.
6. However, your previous records don't have this number.
7. To add a unique clientID, use the 'Replace' command
8. From Browse mode, choose Records -> Show All Records
9. Select the clientID field
10. Choose Records -> Replace Field Contents
11. Select "Replace with serial numbers" and "Update serial number in Entry options"
12. Click Replace

Now that your records have unique identifiers, you'll need to create your new table.

1. File -> Manage -> Databases
2. Select the 'Tables' tab
3. Under 'Table Name', type Monthly Payment
4. Click the fields tab
5. Under 'Field Name', type paymentID, select 'Number' from the Type pop-up menu and select 'Create'
6. Use the options button to make paymentID an auto-enter serial number, just like you did above for clientID
7. Since you're making a relational table, you will also want to turn on "Prohibit modification of value during entry"; this will prevent users (including yourself) from inadvertently modifying the paymentID key field; any modifications will render the relational data useless
8. Click OK to save your changes; you can now create additional fields for your Monthly Payment table, such as Date Paid, Payment Amount and clientID

To view your new table, go to the Layout pop-up menu and select the new 'Monthly Payment' table. From Browse mode, you'll see a message that says 'no records are present'. That's okay; we need to create a relationship first between the two tables. To create a relationship between your two tables using their key fields:

1. File -> Manage -> Database
2. Select the 'Relationships' tab

3. You'll see two different table occurrences, one for the Client Information table and a second for the Monthly Payment table
4. Click and hold the tiny triangle at the bottom of the Client Information table
5. From the Client Information table, click the client field and then drag this to the clientID field in the Monthly Payment table
6. Your tables now have a relationship
7. Double click the box in the middle of the relationship line; the window will now be divided into two halves, one showing the Client Information table, the other showing the Monthly Payment table
8. From the payment side, turn on 'Allow creation of records in this table via this relationship' and 'Delete related records in this table when a record is deleted in the other table'
9. This setup is indicative of a parent-child relationship; you'll be creating your records directly from the Client Information table, and if you delete a record, it will be removed from Monthly Payment (otherwise it would be 'orphaned').
10. Click OK and return to the original Client Information layout.

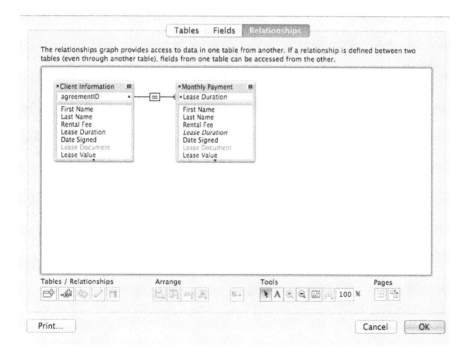

Chapter 4: Creating a Custom Database

Now that you're familiar with how to manage FileMaker, it's time to create your own database! To get started, you'll want to first create fields for storing your data. Next, you'll master the art of controlling layouts so you see only the data you need exactly the way you want.

4.1 Creating the database

To get started, you'll need to tell FileMaker some basic information. When you launch FileMaker, you'll see the Quick Start Screen. If you don't see this, go to the Help menu, select "Quick Start Screen" and choose "Show this screen when FileMaker opens".

1. From the Quick Start Screen, select "Create New Database"
2. Enter a name in the 'Save As' field
3. FileMaker will now launch your brand new database in Table view mode.

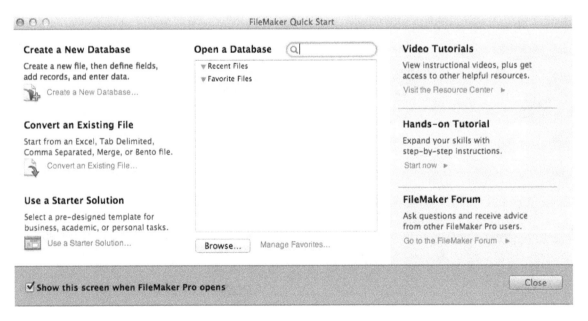

The Quick Start screen

When you first get started, there's not a lot to see. From table view mode, there are just blank fields. You'll need to start creating some. When creating your fields, think about what information your database is built to hold. For example, when creating a client database, you'll need fields for first name, last name, address, email, phone number and more.

1. Create our first field by clicking the 'Create Field' button
2. The button's text will change to 'Field' and the area will be highlighted
3. Type your field's name and press enter
4. You can also hit the "+" sign to save the field and immediately create a new one

TIP: When creating your fields, you'll want to have individually significant data in EACH field. For example, a mailing address typically contains multiple fields, including street name, suite/apt number, city, state and zip code. In order to fully harness the power of FileMaker, you'll need to store all this information in individual fields. Remember, it's always easier to create more fields than you need up front than to split off fields at a later date, especially if you've already made thousands of records.

What are field types?

FileMaker has eight different field types based on the data you put into each field. With the text and number fields, you can store virtually any type of information any way you want. Other fields, such as Date and Time, require information to be entered following a specific format, such as Gregorian dates (11/30/2011) or precise times (11:00pm or 23:00).

While most of the field types are self-explanatory, Container, Calculation and Summary are special fields.

- **Container fields** are used to store files, graphics, movies, sounds or PDFs. These fields have very specific behavior.
- **Calculation fields** are determined by a formula. For example, if you had a field called "Birth Date", then the Calculation field could use a formula to generate age. This is far more effective than manually entering and adjusting ages as time passes. We discussed Calculation fields in 3.6.
- **Summary fields** collect data from across different records. Their value is auto-filled by values from found sets of records. We'll discuss Summary fields in 5.4.

How do I import existing data?

If you have a lot of data in another format, a one-time import from a Microsoft Excel, CSV (comma separated values) or TAB (tab delimited) file will save time.

1. To get started, choose File -> Import Records -> File
2. Select the file and click open
3. Select the destination: for an existing table, choose the table name; for a new table, choose 'new table'
4. If you import to an existing table, use the Import Field Mapping dialog to matching incoming field names with your existing field names
5. Preview imported data by clicking the forwards and backwards arrows below the fields list
6. To create or change import fields, click 'Define Database'
7. Once the fields are properly paired, click Import

4.2 Automatically importing data

FileMaker allows you to automatically import data from a Microsoft Excel, CSV (comma separated values) or TAB (tab delimited) file. Once you setup the import, every time you open your database, FileMaker will automatically import your data. This makes it easy to instantly create sales reports, track workflow and collaborate with coworkers. The source file is automatically imported as a new table into the database. When this occurs, a new layout is also created. You can edit this layout later just as you would any layout that you create in FileMaker.

NOTE: By default, all data imported via recurring import is "Read Only". In order to modify this data, you'll need to go to the "Manage Database" dialog box and uncheck the "Prohibit modification of value during data entry". However, any editing of the data in FileMaker will be overwritten the next time that FileMaker starts. The only way to indefinitely save data associated with an automatic import is to update the source file.

1. In Browse mode, select File -> Import Records -> File
2. Select the file you wish to import
3. Select 'Set up as automatic import'
4. To skip importing column headlines, select 'Don't import first record'
5. From an Excel file, you can import data either by worksheet or by named range
6. Once the import is complete, you can update the data (sync it to its original file) by clicking the script button at the top of the layout screen

4.3 Customizing your database in layout mode

When you create a custom database, you'll also want to customize your database's look and feel. After all, a nice background color and attractive font sure beats staring at a boring grid and Helvetica all day. In layout mode, you can move each object individually, including text, fields and picture objects. You can also add special features to your database, like portals and web viewer (both described below).

To get started, you'll need to switch to layout mode. Once you're here, you'll notice that the different fields in your database all exist as their own entity. If you've ever used a graphic design program or publishing program, Layout mode is very similar to building a publishing document or design. The body controls how much space is devoted to each record. Other parts manage layout features including Title Header, Header, Summary and Footer. You can click and drag each field around to reorder them, change their display sizing and more.

How do I change color, fonts, sizing and other layout elements?

To make design changes, use the Inspector toolbar that will appear on the right of your screen. The Inspector toolbar has three different tabs for managing position, appearance and data. To change the look and feel of your layout, you'll use the appearance tab.

4.4 Conditional formatting

Sometimes you want the formatting of your layout to change depending on certain criteria. For example, if a client is behind on their monthly payments, you might want the monthly payment field to turn red to quickly send a visual indicator about this problem. To add conditional formatting to fields:

1. From List layout, select Status Field
2. Choose Format -> Conditional
3. Click Add
4. From the pop-up menu, make sure that the "Value is" option is chosen
5. From the second menu, choose the condition; for example, you might choose "equal to" or "less than" depending on what data you are trying to highlight
6. From the fill pop-up menu, choose a color
7. Click OK
8. You'll now see a small badge next to your field; this badge signifies that conditional formatting is being used on this field.

4.5 Creating and using portals

Remember how we created a relationship between two tables in Section 3.8 to better manage your clients and monthly payments? When you have related tables, you can create and use portals to manage what information you view in each layout and customize your database.

Here's how.

What is a portal?

A portal lets you see records from other tables in your layout. As the name suggests, it's a hole in your layout that's linked to data from another table. A portal can display as many related records as you want; a portal's capabilities are primarily limited to the size of your layout and the height of your portal.

How do I create a portal?

1. In layout mode, click the Portal tool
2. Click and drag on the layout to create your portal; it may help to imagine that you're drawing a box to be filled with information (since in essence, that's exactly what you are doing)
3. After you draw your box, the Portal Setup dialog appears
4. Choose the table from which you wish to display related records
5. Turn on "Allow deletion of portal records" to ensure synchronicity across your different files
6. Have a lot of information that you need to see? Turn on the "Add Scroll Bar" option to add a scroll bar
7. Select the number or rows you wish your Portal to include

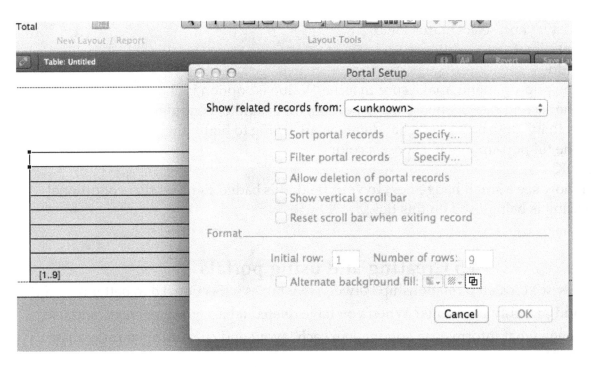

How do I customize my portal?

Once you've added a portal to your layout, you can resize and move this portal just as you would an object. You can also sort the records within your portal. To do so, choose Format -> Portal Setup or double-click your portal. Select the "Sort portal records' option to change the record viewing within your portal. Sorting portal records does not affect your main window's overall sort. FileMaker offers virtually unlimited customization options, so as you get to know the program better, you'll discover even more ways to customize your portals.

How do I control which data is visible through the portal?

Don't want to show all your data? Change the 'initial row value' option. For example, let's say only records 10-20 are of any importance. You can edit your "initial row" value to start at "10" instead of "1", so only the important records are visible.

Can I set my portal to automatically resize?

Yes! Simply anchor the bottom of the portal vertically, and then choose whether you want FileMaker to add more rows or to make each row bigger. If there's any data in the portal that's anchored to the bottom, each portal row will grow and become bigger. If there is no data in the bottom, FileMaker will simply add more rows as the Portal window becomes larger.

4.5 Using the web browser

Imagine your business needs to make several deliveries to your major clients. Trouble is, while you have the address in the database, it would be a lot more convenient to be able to view a map. Switching between FileMaker and Google Maps is time consuming for every client. Plus, what if your addresses change? You need a way to view the map in FileMaker that instantly reflects any record updates. Your solution: Web Viewer Objects.

Does FileMaker have its own web browser?

No. It uses the default browser for whatever operating system you are currently using. For Windows, this is Internet Explorer. For Mac OS X, this is Safari. This means if you install plugins or upgrade your browser, FileMaker will enjoy these same benefits. Plus, you can click on any links you see in the web viewer window and FileMaker will dutifully load the web page.

How does Web Viewer Objects work?

Instead of pulling up a Google map yourself, you can have FileMaker do it for you – or load any web page. Here's how:

1. To get started, you'll need to be in Layout mode; from the toolbar, select the web viewer tool (it's the one that looks like a globe)
2. Click and drag to create a rectangle and tell FileMaker where to put the map
3. Letting go will open the web viewer dialog box
4. From the "Choose Website" list, select Google Maps (US)
5. You'll now need to tell FileMaker where to pull the street address info
6. To the right of the address field, click the square button and choose "specify field"
7. From the specify field window, select the 'Address' option
8. The box will now say Client::Address

Web Viewer Setup

Choose a website and then specify values the website will use to display a web page. Use values from a constant value, or a field or calculated expression. Or, choose Custom Web Address and build your own expression.

Choose a Website

Custom Web Address

Google Maps (US)
Google Maps (CAN)
Google Maps (UK)
MapQuest
Google web search (US)
Google web search (CAN)
Google web search (UK)
Google web search (AU)
Google web search (NZ)
FedEx

Address	Required
Untitled::Address	▸

City	Required
Untitled::City	▸

State	Required
Untitled::State	▸

Zip Code	Optional
Untitled::Zip	▸

Country	Optional
	▸

Web Address

"http://local.google.com/maps?" & "q=" & /*Address=*/ Untitled::Address & "," & /*City=*/ Untitled::City & "," & /*State=*/ Untitled::State & "," & /*Zip Code=*/ Untitled::Zip & "," & /*Country=*/ ""

Specify...

☑ Allow interaction with web viewer content
☐ Display content in Find mode
☑ Display progress bar
☑ Display status messages

Learn More...   Cancel   OK

Web Viewer setup

9. Repeat as necessary to fill in the rest of the address data
10. Click OK
11. Select the web viewer, and anchor it to the right, left and bottom; this will keep it stuck to the bottom of the window and prevent it from bumping into other fields
12. Switch to Browse mode to see your map!

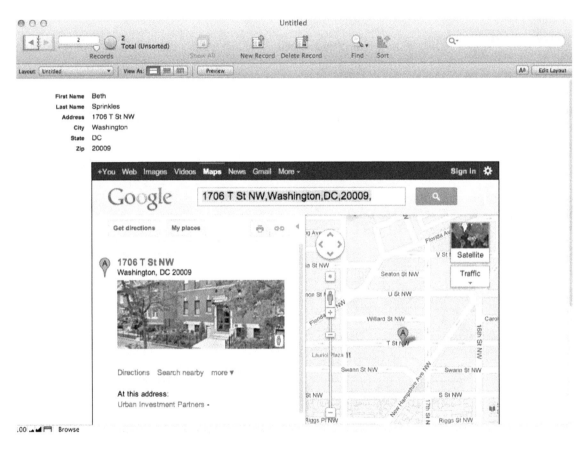

Browse mode showing the web viewer

Chapter 5: Organizing and Editing Records

Now that you've created your custom database, it's time to harness FileMaker's power for organizing, editing and sorting your records.

5.1 Sorting your records

Your old Rolodex could only sort records one way at any given time. If you had the business cards sorted by company, you could not also have them all sorted by last name. Sure, if you only had 10 business cards, resorting was a piece of cake. But what if you had 100 cards? Or 1,000 cards? No one wants to deal with that! FileMaker can sort records any way you want, as many times as you want, including sorting within a sort.

When you first enter your records, you'll notice that the say "unsorted". This means they are organized by "creation order", that is, the first record ever created is listed first, and the most recent record is listed last.

How is sorting different from finding?

Sorting records is different than using the find function. When you find something, you can only see your results in finder. Leave finder view, and you're back to your regular file of every record. Sorting permanently reorganizes all your records based on criteria. For example, let's say you want to sort by last name.

To get started, select Records -> Sort Records, or select the Sort button from the toolbar. This will launch the Sort Records dialog box.

FileMaker will sort based on your criteria. Simply move a field option to the Sort Order box on the right. For a simple alphabetical sort, you'll only need to add one field. For more complex sorts (like by company and last name), the order in which you list each field is the order in which the sort is performed. Listing company first means FileMaker will organize all your contacts by company name, and then list each company member alphabetically by last name. When creating your sort, you can also choose between ascending or descending order.

Is sorting permanent?

When you sort a file, it will remain that way until you return to "creation order" or perform another sort. This means when you close your file and reopen it, the file will be sorted exactly as you left it.

How can I edit my sort?

Simply launch the Sort Records dialog box. You can add new criteria, clear your existing criteria or re-order the criteria. Multi-field sorts can be as complex as you need in order to precisely organize your information.

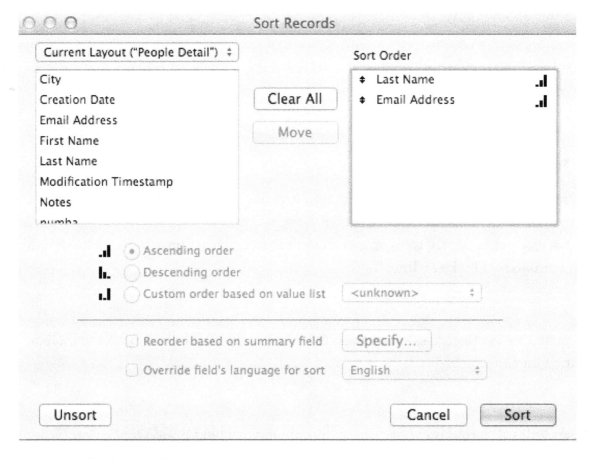

Managing sort order for records

5.2 Sorting with scripts

A script performs tasks for you, essentially doing your grunt work. If you've used Macros before, then you will already be familiar with how a script works. Scripts eliminate the possibility of human error and do things faster.

How do I create a sorting script?

A sort script will automatically sort records for you. Here's how to write a basic alphabetizing script:

1. Choose Records -> Sort records
2. Set up a sort by Last Name followed by First Name
3. Next, choose Scripts -> Manage Scripts
4. The Manage Script dialog will appear
5. Click New and enter a name for your script (e.g., Sort Last Name)
6. In View pop-up menu, choose Found Sets
7. Double-click the Sort Records script
8. Select "Perform without dialog"
9. Select "Specify sort order"
10. Click OK and Save to close and save your script
11. Before closing the Manage Scripts window, check to confirm "Include in Menu" is turned on for your new script

How do I create a button to run my script?

Instead of running your script from a menu, you can run it directly from a button

1. In Layout mode, select the "Last Name" field by clicking on the label
2. Choose Format -> Button Setup
3. Select Perform Script
4. Select your new "Sort Last Name" script

Once you've got your new button created, be sure to apply formatting to indicate to your users that your button does something useful!

How do I apply a script trigger?

Script triggers give you an automated way to run a script without even needing to press a button. For example, a script trigger like "Sort by Last name" will execute this command every time you view the layout from Browse mode, instantly allowing you to view a layout just how you want, without bothering to sort it yourself.

5.3 Advanced Find techniques

In 3.4, we covered the basics of a FileMaker search. But if you have thousands of records in your database, a simple search is not going to cut it. Here's how to locate the data you need as efficiently as possible.

How can I access my last search?

FileMaker always keeps track of your most recent search, whether it's been minutes or weeks since you last ran the find. To access this, choose Records -> Modify Last Find. This will automatically bring up your last found set of records, which is helpful if you can't remember the search criteria you used to find something. In addition to the records, your search criteria will be sitting right there, too.

How do I constrain or extend my search?

Each time you perform a find, FileMaker forgets the previous search and produces a brand new set. But what if you wanted to constrain your existing set (add further search restrictions) or extend your set (add new data to the set that matches a different set of criteria)? Constraining a set is just like doing an "And" search after the fact. Here's how:

1. Perform your normal search
2. Switch to Find mode
3. Type your new search term
4. Choose Requests -> Constrain Found Set

Extending a set is like doing an "Or" search after the fact. Here's how:

1. Perform your name search
2. Switch to Find mode
3. Type or select your new search term
4. Choose Requests -> Extend Found Set

How do I use search operators?

FileMaker uses 17 different search operators to refine searches. For example, let's say you're searching for the word "land" in the places field. A simple "land" search will turn up the location "Land 'o Lakes" but overlook Disneyland. To tell FileMaker that you're searching for the word wherever it appears in the field (not just by itself), you'll need to use a search operator. In this example, you'll want to use the Wildcard operator (*) by typing *land*. You can also type *land to find anything that ends in land or land* to find anything that starts with land. A list of the 17 operators is below.

< Less Than - Find all records that are less than specified value

≤ Less Than Or Equal - Find all records that are less than or equal to specified value

> Greater Than - Find all records that are greater than specified value.

≥ Greater Than Or Equal - Find all records that are greater than or equal to specified value

= Exact Match - Match the search term exactly

... Range - Find records between two different values in a field

! Duplicates - Find records that have exactly matching data within the search field, such as duplicate contact records in an address database

// Today's Date – Find records that match today's date (e.g., every payment that is due today); simply enter the character, no additional information is necessary

? Invalid Date or Time – Find records that are supposed to hold a date or time, rather than 'N/A' or 'Next Week'; simply enter the character, no additional information is necessary

@ One Character Wildcard – One character wildcard search (e.g., "Da@" finds "Dad" or "Dan" but not "Dave")

* Unlimited Character Wildcard – Unlimited wildcard search (e.g., "Da@" finds "Dad", "Dan", "Dave" and "Danielle")

"""" Literal Text – Find text exactly as you enter it

~ The Relaxed Search – This only applies to Japanese text files, searching for characters to match a sound even if they aren't the same character (kind of like searching for "fat" and also getting results with the term "phat", but this search tool only applies to Japanese characters!)

== Field Content Match – Find exact matches to what you type; exact same words in the exact order

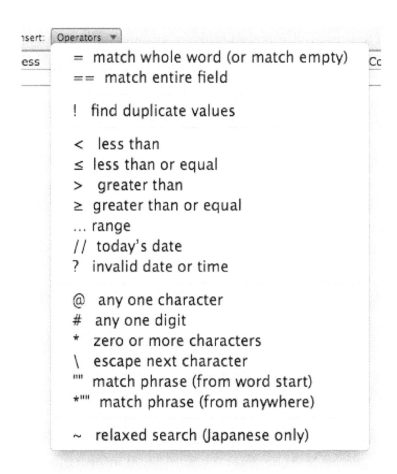

Search operators

NOTE: You can make your searches even more powerful by mixing and matching your search terms. For example, you can use ">//" to search for all payments that are due after today's date or all orders scheduled for delivery after today's date.

How do I search for duplicate records?

Sooner or later, you'll end up with duplicate records in your database. For example, a client database may have the same client multiple times, but with different addresses and phone numbers. Or maybe you updated the phone number in one record, but not in the next. If you search ONLY for duplicate records by putting the ! operator in every field, you won't turn up the records that are essentially the same save for a simple typo or entry mistake. Try putting the ! operator in as few fields as possible, such as just the first and last name.

How do I search for a specific term that is also an operator?

FileMaker uses common symbols as operators. Sometimes, however, these symbols (especially '@') will be included in the term you want to search. Simply typing 'name@mail.com', however, will not bring up your email address. FileMaker will think that you are performing a one-character wildcard search. Instead, you'll need to ???

5.3 Saving and recreating finds

How do I save a find?

When you perform a find that you may need to use again, you'll want to save it. To do so, select Find -> Save Current Find. Enter the find name and choose save. NOTE: Saved finds are specific to your file; you'll only be able to see your finds when you are logged in under the account with which you created the finds.

How do I edit a saved find?

To edit a saved find, select Records -> Saved Finds -> Edit Saved Finds. The "Edit Saved Finds" dialog box will show all your saved finds. Simply select the one you wish to modify and hit 'Edit'. Need to preserve the original find and also make modifications? Select 'Duplicate' to create a duplicate find for editing purposes.

How do I recreate a find?

Forgot to hit save? All is not lost. One of the fastest ways to recreate a find is by using the Find pop-up menu. The Find pop-up menu appears when you hold the mouse down on the Find icon rather than clicking it. You'll see a list of recent finds and saved finds.

5.4 Organizing by summaries and sub-summaries

What is a summary field?

One of the most important fields included in a report is the summary field. (See Section 6 for in-depth reporting.) A summary field is different from other fields because it is not associated with a specific record. Instead, a summary field processes data from multiple records. Summary fields carry out basic commands, such as total, average, count, minimum, maximum, standard deviation, etc. You can also choose whether you want your summary field to be a "running count" or to "restart" the count for each sorted group. The real power of the Summary field lies when you use it in conjunction with the "Sub-summary" function. For example, this will let you have a count of clients by state, and then a further sub-summary by zip code or city.

How do I create a summary field?

For example, let's say you want a count of all the clients in your database. You'll create a summary field to do this.

1. From your database, choose File -> Manage -> Database
2. From the database window, choose the Fields tab
3. Type "ClientCount"
4. From the type pop-up menu, select Summary -> Create
5. From the Summary dialog box, choose the type of field you need to create; in this case, it's a "Count of".
6. From the Available Fields list, choose the field you wish to summarize; in this case, it's "LastName"
7. Click OK, FileMaker will add the new field to your field list.

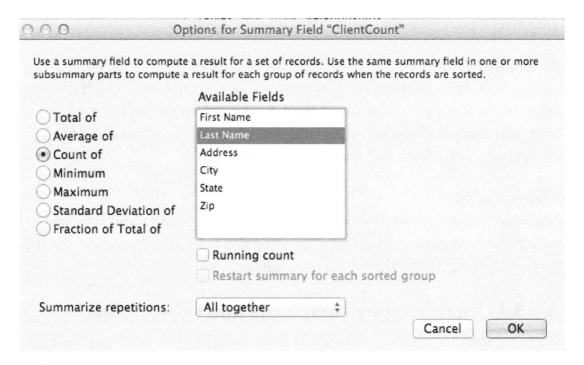

Creating a summary field

How do I create a sub-summary?

1. Once you have a summary field created, you can use that field to create sub-summaries
2. In Layout mode choose Insert -> part

3. Select the "sub-summary when sorted by" option
4. From the field list, select the desired field; in this case, it's "State"
5. Click OK and then choose whether you want this sub-summary to appear at the top or the bottom of your record totals
6. If you select "Print Above", FileMaker will add a new Sub-summary part to the layout between the header and body

When you return to layout view, you'll see summary and sub-summary parts stacked on top of each other, just like this:

Sub-summary field in Layout mode

When you switch to Browse mode, your layout will look just like it always did. You'll need to switch to State or Zip Code to show the groups and totals. You can always change the sorting order from Layout mode.

Chapter 6: Creating Reports & Charts

6.1 Understanding reports

Now that you've built a powerful database, it's time to harness this power to analyze your data. One of the easiest ways to analyze data is by producing reports. A report is a dynamic data analysis based on specific criteria. Every time you add new records to your file, this will be reflected in your report.

6.2 Creating a report

1. In Layout mode, choose Layouts -> New Layout/Report
2. From the "Show records from" pop-up menu, choose your master table. In this example, we'll use our Client Information table again
3. Select a layout type
4. The sample report will dynamically adjust as you make additions/modifications; when you are satisfied, click 'Next'
5. From the specify fields menu, select the fields you want to include in your report (such as First Name, Last Name, Payment Due, etc.), click Next
6. From the Organize Records by Category menu, arrange the categories so your report makes sense; for example, you will list Last Name and First Name under the 'Sort order' list
7. You can also specify what you'd like for subtotals and the summary field; the summary field counts each record in the sorted category group and displays a count of the sorted records for each group

How does subtotaling work?

Subtotals let you create separate subsets within the report. For example, let's say you wanted a report the listed all your clients alphabetically, along with the total amount they've spent in the last year. You might find it helpful to further break this report down by spending subcategories. For example, you could specify a range for your big spenders and have any records that fall in this range listed first; a second tier would be for middle-spenders and a final tier for low spenders. Within each tier your client records would be organized alphabetically. To do this, you'll need to use the specify subtotals tool from the New Layout/Report dialog box.

1. Choose category to summarize by and select your category; in this case, it's annual spending

2. Choose 'Subtotal placement' to select where to place this subtotal in relation to the record group
3. Click 'Add'; doing so will bring you to the 'Specify Field' window
4. You can choose between a 'running count' or 'restart summary for each sorted group'

How can I make my reports automatic?

Specifying report parameters can be time consuming. When you've got everything just right, select the 'Create a script' option from the report menu.

1. Type the name of your report into the "Script name" box, such as Client Spending.
2. Select 'Run script automatically' and click next
3. FileMaker will automatically write you a script for creating your report; now every time you open the report, FileMaker will run the script and automatically update the report based on your records. That was easy!

6.3 Customizing report layout

Sadly, after all that hard work, your new report doesn't look that special. In fact, from a graphic design stand point, FileMaker reports look a bit tragic when they're first generated. Using your Layout design skills, however, you polish this report up.

Why do layouts matter?

Layouts give your data visual structure. A few minutes spent tweaking the fonts, adding color or even pasting in your logo for company branding will make your business look professional. This also makes it easy to hand out your report to clients or at meetings.

How do I use the Layout bar?

The Layout bar is located between the Status toolbar and the Content Area of your window. To get started, click the 'Edit Layout' button. From edit layout mode, you'll notice that the menu and command options have changed. Even icons that look the same have changed their function. For example, the book icon lets you flip through different layouts rather than flipping through each record.

The layout toolbar

NOTE: If you can't see the Layout bar, this may be because the Status toolbar is hidden. Click the Status toolbar button at the bottom of your window. If you're a Mac user, you can toggle the toolbar on and off by clicking the oblong button in the upper-right corner of the window.

What are Layout objects?

Layout objects are the basic building blocks for any layout, such as text objects, lines, shapes and images. Clicking any object allows you to move it, resize it and apply formatting. Use the Format Painter tool to copy formatting from one object to the next of the same type. Just like with text or images, you can apply formatting rules to field objects.

6.4 Creating charts

A chart turns your dry data into a visually engaging and quick-to-understand form. While summary reports are great, there will come a time when you'll yearn for the classic pie chart or bar chart. Fortunately, FileMaker makes creating these charts easy. You can choose from five basic charts: bar, horizontal bar, line, area and pie.

1. To get started, you'll need to be in Layout mode
2. Select Chart tool, and then drag to create a chart using most of the space below the fields
3. This will launch the Chart setup dialog box
4. From here you can choose the chart type, enter a title, select the horizontal and vertical axis and choose where to pull your data

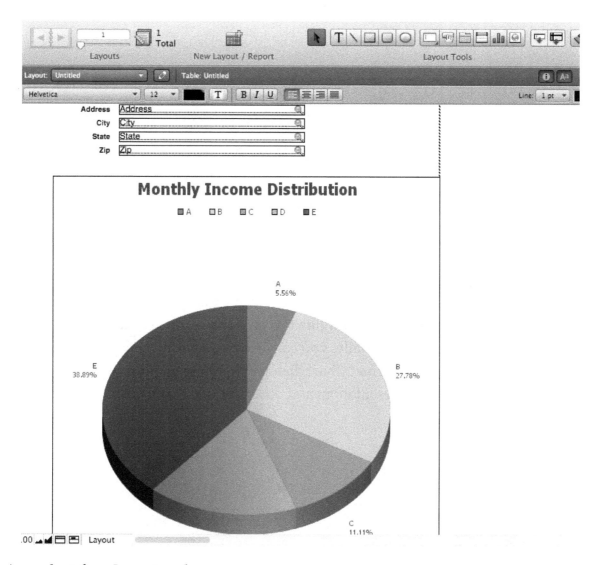

Viewing a chart from Layout mode

My chart is squished and missing labels – how do I fix this?

Once you create a chart, you may notice some problems. Is your axis missing a unit of measurement? Do the labels overlap? Does your entire chart appear to be squished? From layout mode, click on the chart to select it. From the Inspector window, choose "Position" and under Auto-sizing, activate the bottom and right anchors. When all four anchors are active, your chart will stretch to fill the size of the window.

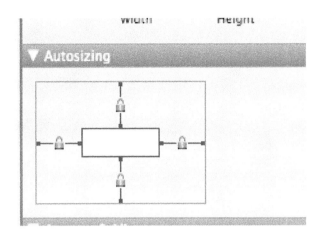

Activate all four anchors under autosizing on the Inspector window

To fix other formatting issues, select Format -> Chart Setup. From here, you can make formatting changes, such as turning the labels to a 45-degree angle (which will solve the issue of overlapping labels), change the label and title text size and color, and adjust the max/min numbers to set the axis label range. Finally, you can also change font, color scheme and background options through the Format Chart dialog box. These include switching between a solid or shaded color, flat or 3D presentation, and other options that vary based on the type of chart.

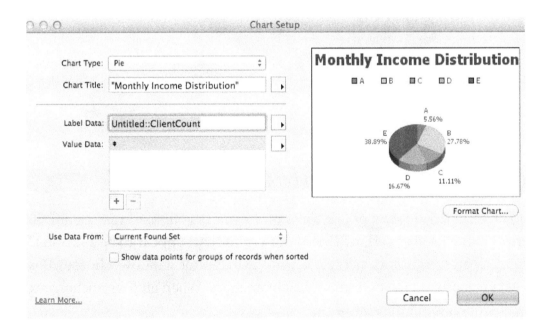

6.6 Tips for creating a meaningful chart
Keep these tips in mind when creating a chart that not only looks good but also makes sense

for your data.

- Time goes on the X-axis (horizontal axis)
- Numerical values go on the Y-axis (vertical axis)
- Multiple Y values are part of a series. If you have multiple series, a good option is to use a line graph to compare performances over time.
- Choose a pie chart to show percentages of a whole; for example, if you want to compare which parts of your business generate the most revenue, the entire pie is your total revenue while each slice represents a component of your business (e.g.: phone sales, in-person sales, internet sales, etc.)

Chapter 7: Sharing and Protecting Your Database

One of FileMaker's best features is the ability to share a database with multiple users. There are three types of sharing: FileMaker Network, Internet Sharing and FileMaker Server. FileMaker Server is a program that's built for large-scale database hosting. This guide will focus on using FileMaker Network and Internet Sharing.

7.1 FileMaker Network sharing

The easiest way to share your database is through your office network. To do so, you'll need to ensure that all your database files are on your computer. Next, you'll name your computer the host. Each computer that opens one of your files will be called a guest. Up to nine guests can connect to one host at a single time. Once you have network sharing setup, everyone will be able to add, edit, and delete records, as well as perform finds, run scripts and print. However, no two people can modify the same record at the same time. Depending on user privileges, you may even be able to write scripts, work in layout mode, etc. Even with shared administrative privileges, only one person at a time can edit a script or layout, or use the Manage -> Database window.

How do I turn on network sharing?

File-> Sharing-> FileMaker Network

How do I tell FileMaker which databases to share?

Under FileMaker Network, select the setting dialog box. You'll see a list of sharing options.

1. From the "currently open files" list, select a database
2. Choose from the following settings:
   - All Users – Anyone on your Network with FileMaker can use the database
   - Privilege Set – Specify which users have access on your network
   - No Users – Keep the file private and only accessible to the host

How do I access a shared file?

One of the easiest ways to access a shared file is by having your coworker send you a link to the file. Your coworker can go to File -> Send -> Link to Database. You can also access a file remotely on your own. Choose File -> Open Remote, select the Host, and select the file.

7.2 FileMaker Internet Sharing: Instant Web Publishing (IWP)

You can also use Instant Web Publishing to share your database online with users that don't have FileMaker Pro. IWP turns your computer into a server and your layouts into web pages. Your online databases will work and look just like FileMaker Pro on your desktop, allowing anyone with a browser the ability to search, sort and edit data directly.

How do I turn on web sharing?

File -> Sharing -> Instant Web Publishing. This will display a URL for you to send to other users to access your database. By default, FileMaker uses the web publishing port 80. If you don't have any other web services running on your computer, port 80 won't be a problem. But if you do, you can use FileMaker's special port number, 591, to avoid conflict. If you use 591, you'll also need to tell other users this port number. You'll share the link as: http://mycomputer:591"/.

How do I manage what information FileMaker shares?

Under Advanced Web Publishing options, you can control who access your information. After all, you may not want just anyone finding your computer. From the Advance Web Options dialog box, select the "Accessible only from these IP addresses" option. You can specify a range of IP addresses that are acceptable, such as 192.168.0.10*. From the Advanced Web Publishing options, you can also select the "Disconnect inactive accounts" option; this will automatically log anyone out who has not been recently active.

How do I access the database via the web?

Simply enter the link into your URL box. FileMaker will prompt you to login to the database. If you have not set up a password, you can login using 'Admin' as the user name and leaving the password blank.

7.3 Record locking

When we first discussed how to create records, we said that the record was locked until it was committed to the database. Record locking means that if you have a record open, no one else can make edits or access that record. In the case of shared databases, if you try to edit a locked record, you'll receive a message that someone else is using it (you'll see both the computer user name and the account name).

While record locking can be a minor annoyance for data entry, it can be a serious problem for scripts. If everyone has the same privileges, these means multiple people can run the same script at the same time (well, try to run the script!) For example, let's say you wrote a script to manage flagged records. If multiple people are flagging different records and then both try to run the script, FileMaker will become completely confused. In general, it's best to only allow one person the privilege to run certain scripts in order to prevent database chaos.

7.4 FileMaker Security

FileMaker allows you to manage WHO can access a database and WHAT each person can do once he or she is in your database.

What is a privilege set?

As the database creator, you can also create user accounts for each person who needs to access your database. You control what they can and cannot do through privilege sets. We advise only giving someone the exact privileges they need to get the job done. For example, if your client database also has a list of credit card numbers, the last thing you want to do is give your entire team access to exporting these numbers – or you may find yourself on the wrong end of a criminal fraud investigation one day.

Every database comes with three built-in privilege set levels: Full Access, Data Entry Only and Read-Only Access. You can also create custom privilege sets. By default, each privilege set that you create starts out with no privileges; you'll have to manually add each one. To speed this process up, you can also choose to an existing access set such as "Data Entry Only", duplicate it and then fine-tune the privileges from here.

What type of privileges can I control?

You can manage virtually every privilege – from printing and exporting to overriding data validation warnings and even allowing users to modify their own password. It's all at your discretion.

How do I create a privilege set?

1. File -> Manage Security
2. Click New
3. Type the Privilege Set Name, a description and then select the different checkboxes for giving the user privilege (such as printing reports)
4. Select 'Data Access and Design' from the privilege dialog box to manage access to records, layouts, value lists, scripts and more

When editing privilege sets, you'll often choose between "all modifiable" (run and edit), "all executable" (run only) "all no access" (cannot do anything) and a custom-privilege box, where you can fully customize accessibility.

How do I edit a privilege set after it's created?

Change your mind about access? Have you added new features to the database and need to manage their privileges? Return to the 'Manage Security' window and select your privilege set name. NOTE: You cannot edit the privilege levels that come built-in with FileMaker (Full Access, Data Entry Only and Read-Only Access); if you need to tweak these, duplicate them first.

How do I create a user account?

Now that you've created a privilege set, you're ready to create a user account!

1. File -> Manage Security
2. Click New
3. Type the Account name
4. Enter a password
5. Select the privilege set

New accounts default to active. If an employee leaves your company, you can use this menu to make her account inactive.

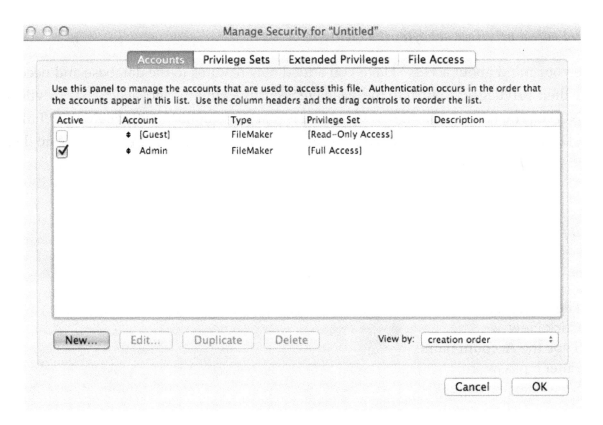

Managing account security: note the options at the top for switching between accounts, privilege sets, extended privileges and file access

Chapter 8: FileMaker Go for iPhone and iPad

8.1 FileMaker Go Overview

FileMaker Go is a FileMaker app for iPhone and iPad. It's designed as an on-the-go solution for inventory management, sales and more. For example, you can use it to conduct an inventory check on-site, generate sales orders when visiting your customers, tracking shipping, update project statuses while traveling, and add research notes from the field.

As far as business apps go, FileMaker Go is pretty powerful. Now you can take your database with you wherever you go. Copy databases and email them straight from your iPad. View, edit and search for your information. Add, modify or delete records in your database. Features including QuickFind, Web Viewer and FileMaker charts all work in FileMaker Go. Plus, you can take advantage of iOS 5's AirPrint feature to print charts and reports wherever you are.

8.2 Getting started - iPad

To get started, you'll need to download FileMaker Go for the iPad. By default, FileMaker Go features a basic two-column interface. On the left side, you'll see files that are on your iPad. On the right side, you'll see a list of remote files and hosts, including recently opened files.

How do I manage multiple windows?

To open a file, simply tap the file you wish to view. When you open a file, you notice that the navigational controls are largely spread out in the corners of the interface. This is different from FileMaker Pro, which clusters the tools together. However, this style is consistent with other iOS 5 applications, and makes for an intuitive and user-friendly interface. In the upper left corner is the "file window manager". This allows you to see the different windows you are currently viewing. To add a new window, tap the window manager and tap the green + button. To close a window, tap the red X. Use your finger to swipe between different windows and tap to select. By default, file manager is your home screen. If you close all your windows, you'll end up back here.

How do I change my layout or viewing options?

To switch between different layout options, use the gear icon in the top right corner. Tap the 'Select Layout' option to switch between record view, record list and other summary layouts you may have created, such as an inventory report. Tap "View As" to choose between form, list or table, just like in FileMaker Pro. You can also quickly change your layout selection by tapping the 'Record Detail' button at the bottom left of the screen. This will open the same menu of viewing choices.

How do I sort or find records?

Use the sort/find records button located in the bottom right of the screen. You'll have access to basic sorting and finding functions, including the ability to find, omit, sort, enter find mode and perform a QuickFind.

8.3 Getting started - iPhone

To get started, you'll need to download FileMaker Go for the iPhone. By default, FileMaker Go features a recent files navigation screen, which is essentially a list of files you recently opened. Since the iPhone offers less screen real estate than the iPad, this view (and other screen views) will be different from what you see on the iPad. All files are listed together, including local files and hosted files.

How do I manage my windows?

While the viewing screen may look different to accommodate the iPhone, the same navigational corners that exist on the iPad also exist on the iPhone. To open a file, simply tap the file you wish to view. When you open a file, you notice that the navigational controls are located at the corners of the interface. In the upper left corner is the "file window manager". This allows you to see the different windows you are currently viewing. To add a new window, tap the window manager and tap the green + button. To close a window, tap the red X. Use your finger to swipe between different windows and tap to select. By default, file manager is your home screen. If you close all your windows, you'll end up back here.

How do I change my layout or viewing options?

To switch between different layout options, use the tool icon in the top right corner. Tap the 'Select Layout' option to switch between record view, record list and other summary layouts you may have created, such as an inventory report. Tap "View As" to choose between form, list or table, just like in FileMaker Pro. You can also quickly change your layout selection by tapping the 'Record Detail' button at the bottom left of the screen. This will open the same menu of viewing choices. Unlike the iPad, the iPhone does not automatically show scroll control for easy scrolling through your records. You'll need to tap the record first to activate the scroll control bar.

How do I sort or find records?

Use the sort/find records button located in the bottom right of the screen. You'll have access to basic sorting and finding functions, including the ability to find, omit, sort, enter find mode and perform a QuickFind.

How do I add or delete records?

Tap the +/- button at the bottom of the screen to launch a menu with instructions to add or delete a record.

8.4 Syncing files – iPhone & iPad

While the viewing options may differ slightly between the iPhone and iPad, both devices send, save and sync files the same way.

How do I add local files?

To add local files, you will need to connect your iPhone or iPad to the computer using iTunes. Once your iPhone or iPad is connected, simply drag and drop the files, just as you would with any document file. You can also email yourself (or have someone else email you) a FileMaker Pro database. As long as you have FileMaker Go, you'll be able to open it directly on your iPhone or iPad. To synch your changes with the desktop, simply connect your device to your computer or email your database file.

How do I add a host for remote files?

From file browser, select the "Add Hosts" option under "Favorite Hosts". Enter your remote hosting information. Your business will need to be running FileMaker Server for this feature to work. Otherwise, you'll need to manually send and synch your own files.

How do I refresh network files?

If you're on the go, your files are only as good as the last time you updated them. Keep them fresh by using the "Refresh Window" feature. Under settings, tap "Refresh Window". This will cause FileMaker Go to dump its current cache and retrieve an updated file from the server.

How do I save changes back to the server?

With FileMaker Pro, every change is automatic; there's no need to "save" anything. As long as you are connected to Wi-Fi or a 3G network, your changes will be automatically synched back to the master database.

How do I save or email a copy of the database?

The Save/Send menu option is located under the Settings menu. Tap this option to save a copy of your database or to email a copy. To save a file as a PDF, go to Settings -> Print and select the PDF option.

Conclusion

FileMaker Pro is a powerful program with great flexibility to scale up or scale down depending on your business's needs. This guide covered the fundamentals to getting started: introducing you to the layout and different viewing modes, the basics of data entry and automatic import, and how to customize the look and feel of your database. We also discussed the basics of searching and filtering information, as well as how to refine your search using operators.

Now that you've mastered the basics (and a few advanced tasks, too), you'll find that it's easy to use and follow FileMaker's impressive collection of online documentation. As your database skills grow, you'll create more advanced scripts and calculations for managing basic tasks and even use developer utilities to create a fully custom display that's eye-catching, intuitive and easy-to use. As you become a power developer, you may also want to join one of the local user groups or email lists. Check out http://www.filemaker.com/support/mailinglists.html for a full list of forums, email lists and newsgroups to inspire your developer skills!

About Minute Help Press

Minute Help Press is building a library of books for people with only minutes to spare. Follow @minutehelp on Twitter to receive the latest information about free and paid publications from Minute Help Press, or visit minutehelpguides.com.